THE LAMENTS OF THE SOUL

Thirty-two prose poems

USE ALL THE WORDS & DO NOT BLAME THEM FOR THE WEIGHT OF THE WORLD •

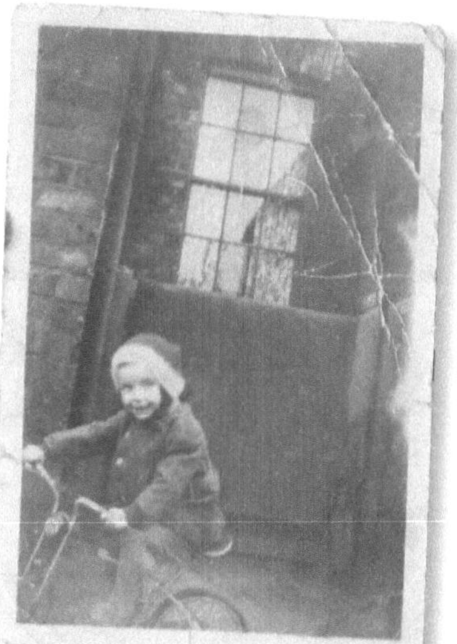

THE LAMENTS OF THE SOUL

Thirty-two prose poems

Writing No.14

PETER HAGUE

The Laments of the Soul

First Published in Autumn 2023
by Peter Hague Concept Design Art Direction

ISBN 978-1-7394388-0-7

Cover Design, layout and the illustration on page 30/31 is by Peter Hague Concept Design Art Direction.

Additional editing: Lara Newton
Additional photography and pink metal pig locator:
Judith McGarry.

Also available in hardback: ISBN 978-1-7394388-1-4

A catalogue record for this book
is available from the British Library.

Also by Peter Hague

Writing No.8
Hope in the Heart of Hatred
Poems of Experience Soul and Defiant Spirit
Twenty-nine poems

Writing No.10
Gain of Function
One hundred and two poems

Writing No.11
Summer With The Gods
Seventy-three poems

Writing No.12
Louder Prayers
Seventy-one poems

Writing No.13
The Momentary Clock
Seventy-six poems

Writing No.14
The Laments of the Soul
Thirty-two prose poems

Writing No.15
No Road Home
The Enormous Journey of Guilt
Seventy-eight poems

To Betty and Herbert

CONTENTS

part one

A WAYWARD SON

part two

DISTORTED HORIZONS

CONTENTS

part three

OBSERVATIONS FROM THE GAME

part four

RETURN OF THE NIGHTWATCHMAN

INTRODUCTION

"And on that whim (and once again) I slipped my Mother's grasping hand and ran outside. An infant, finding my own way home."

This experimental work of prose poetry has me seeking a new range of poetic expression, one that crosses the familiarity of truncated lines and finds a different way to control the words, for example: the three lines italicised above are an edit from the end of the main flow of the third poem in this book. I reprise it here as a demonstration of the dynamic form I am exploring. And although it may seem at first that these poems are more verbose than my normal style, this is not actually true. There were many such edits of beautiful lines like these that were disregarded in favour of better flow and concise story telling. Overall, I am pleased with the outcome and I am sure my readers will feel the same.

The book is my usual take on the various difficulties life throws our way, though it is powerful too, a feature that is indicative of the special flow and tight nature of the working of the subject matter. I do not promote political themes in any way than merely 'said' or 'balanced'. And that is not done to weaken any words or their strength of delivery or my conviction; it mainly comes from a natural stance of being fair, and by the same token, they are *merciless* when necessary. I have no time for the crazy views that poison our world and I can be quite vociferous when it comes to dispatching or supporting them. It should be said though that not all life's questions are answerable – some will never be defined, simply because the other viewpoint may have been established first, leaving no return from its control – we would need a whole new civilisation for that.

It is always wise to test, and sometimes deny, certain standards that have held true in those many regions of our lives that are vulnerable to undeniable change. With this in mind, do not lean on the loyalty of your predecessors; they nurtured you in very different times, hoping you would be wise enough to find the best ways and beliefs for yourself in a constantly uncertain future, at the same time supporting the core of their simple truth, and the wisdom of their sometimes accidentally complex foundations. They are still at the very heart of it all and willing you on. Learn from your trials and flex the various laments that hide in your souls.

THE LAMENTS OF THE SOUL

Thirty-two prose poems

*Let us confound the powers that be
and decide to live in peace.*

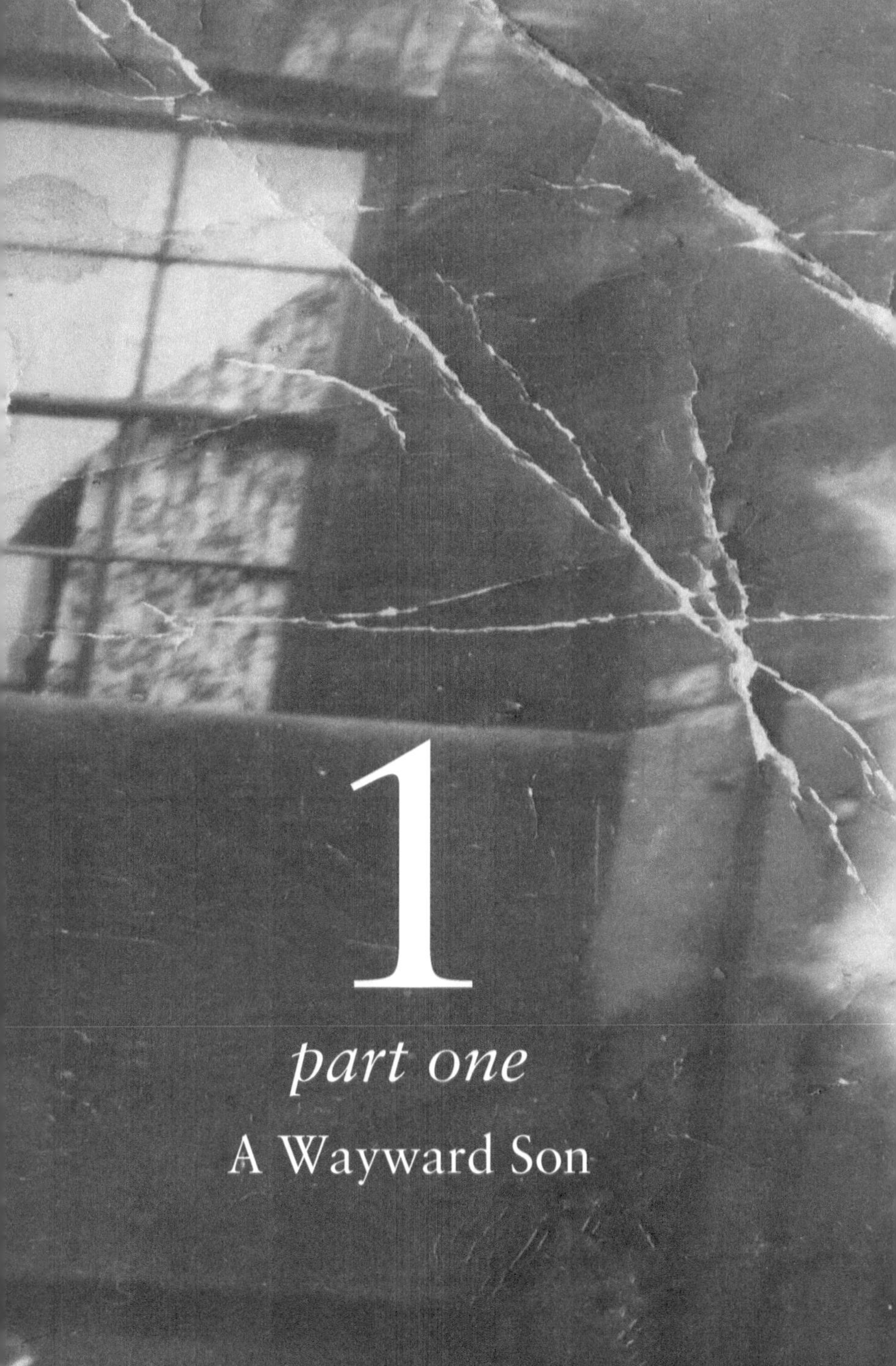

1

part one

A Wayward Son

I

The Seductive Pool

Quantum me.

Out in the street with rain and liars, we are forced into a culture of begging and commerce. It wants us to rely on a competence of control from the mesmerising shade of card-shark hands. They need you more than you need them; they need the infantry of tax-payers dollars – and a piece of your house – the soldier you – the what they call: 'the lesser men'. They need you to thrust your hands into ignorant pockets, with a certain level of permitted dismay. And to shrug your shoulders in consenting indifference, where darkening skies need not be your burden. They need you to tip the economy in their favour, with its designated scroll of smouldering credit – to cast it into the lining of their chestnut suits and the towering laws that support their vices. Their world is about money and controlling power – and robot sex beyond sex's reach. They lean on their riches to force a breach into the charted ecstasy of artificial minds – an uncertain love, needing no feelings.

continued...

I cannot think of anything reliable now; everything pays for their deliberate research. The shops are broken and the roads misleading – and governance has grown too wide to be certain – too wide for the simple strings of democracy to work. They have sown the seeds of apologetic thinking; cast under a muted breath of heaving despair. Only those listening may dismiss the call – a subliminal wink behind the eyes of friends to reinforce the none-importance of it all.

I have tuned my eyes to the proportions of a colossus, which offers no measurement that agrees with physics. For my eyes are spaced miles apart, and I am tuning them for sound, as a radio telescope. In fact, I can see around the back of my head to a blurred map hanging on a crumbling wall – or is that just a failing waterfall? It is hard to tell, using the resolution of a graph, with its zig-zag of washed-out particles of light – the collapsed wave being the last thing I see, before the superposition of *myself* and *me*. The experiment seems a partial success, but there is less detail of what lies ahead – the more we see of the micro-view, the more elusive becomes the key – and frankly, I still have no desirable evidence to place alongside the undesirable clue.

Mine eyes have seen the glory… but there are no confirmed experimental results. I tried to find that simple room where the truth is easy, but I failed once more. I think it is behind the falling gloom, that collapses into a multiple fate – but only because I hailed it so, like a cab, as it moved towards my static state – stopping at the dual entanglement of my feet. I was confused, it being unimaginable in direction – refusing like an automaton to offer *position* without *validation*. But how can things stand still while representing velocity of mind? It was a valid attempt to get me re-instated – for I am not welcome now in quantum physics – I have been disowned by my own equations – but at least I can claim that glorious outcome and call it true.

I will put my face forward again some day – like a swimmer looking for the human clue. I will swim for miles and miles across my cosmic carpet and always be a 'who'. And being unmeasurable, I will be the pool of myself – not quite welcome in the liquefaction of time. My expanding thoughts will not demand glory, being the result of mere elegance and a duality of grace.

II
Exotic

Be careful of wishes.

Be careful where you go with Exotic. Be careful how you court it. It will soon be the mayor of your crumbling town, and worse – it will no longer be your town. Exotic will forget you nurtured it – that you were the soul champion of its dark virtue. It will start to believe you had no choice against inevitable supremacy, and its directive to suppress, using a unique version of truth. You enriched it only through subjugation – a clever ploy – but only to the fool. Soon there is something like swastika flags hanging above the entrance to the hollow town hall – and nationalist wallpaper, made of inviting maps, now stretch beyond the hints of your local territory.

Exotic lives around the corner from idealism. And near the blandishments of your peaceful religion – a place where people start to disappear – and many mysteries occur that you will not want unfolded. The secret of your church is already a broken wonder, embarrassed by its collection of unburied bones. But you cannot be choosey – it becomes all or nothing – a toleration of that which does not tolerate anything – and you cannot make it better praying for transferable enlightenment – the exotic deviance has written its laws based on a foundation of idealist troubles. They meet each week in the courtyard, to enforce them. I will see you there, nodding like a pleasant fool, just before your head comes loose – the headless fool you were born to be, and that *Exotic* always knew you were.

Exotic spied your weakness from afar – an addled tear in the conquering hero's eyes. Now its monsters have risen to even the score and philosophy will not help your concerned expression – philosophy has never been equipped to defuse cultures into a liberal map of the human race. There are too many oddments to lash together, it would creak at best, like an old ship – it would lack the engine of inherent grace. You will realise this much too late – after you have set sail to be buried at sea, having lost sight of your once, beloved land.

III
A Visit to Dr Ninian Dick

The beginnings of a dangerous life. 1956

"And on that whim (and once again) I slipped my Mother's grasping hand and ran outside. An infant, finding my own way home."

In an embellished room and a time you will not know, I waited to see my doctor, amidst a musical of chairs. There was a Persian carpet and velvet drapes – sumptuous as the oil paintings, glowing in their gilded frames. These classical distractions of seascapes and traditional themes were hung from the blessing of a stout picture-rail – and with all the authority of chains.

I was sitting with my Mother in 1956, when medicine was almost fake, but well presented – even in a town built of smoke and terraced streets. I watched a noble clock, ticking to the stride of a swinging spoon. It scribed its arc beneath the glorious arms of a chandelier – a fairground-ride, that embraced the dark with its fashioned light – and there was a certain amount of fear; a trepidation that circled the room – as cautious as a fox might. It passed quietly from one face to another; a parcel of frowns for the doctor to unravel – yet this was carried ever-forward in a respectable silence that the clock's momentum failed to break. There was no sound louder – no silence as deeply opaque.

The door was opened by the doctor himself, who invited my name to challenge his skill. He was a tall Scottish man, wearing a royal blue suit, who knew where I lived, being present at my birth – I was born in the front bedroom of a terraced house, a few years back and three streets down the road. Dr Ninian Dick lived above his office, with the success of respect surrounding this noble abode. His was a corner house, across from the park – smothered in trees – yet looking four ways – pointing my blatant temptation toward home through this natural confluent of desire and escape. It was a Victorian presence at the crossroads of life, wearing the eager growth of an industrial town. On general visits, he carried a full bag of confidence, shining out of the mystery of a leather case. A well travelled baggage, now

continued...

resting closed, within a designated position on the monolith of his desk.

The axel of his surgery had become an empirical hub, turning with the austere mood of my serious neighbourhood. It was a human foundry of mystery and charade, and with the official walls of panelled wood. Beneath the Highland landscape of moors and grouse I saw the threatening spectre of stainless steel, all forged within the sterility of surgical glass and the bland surfaces of white enamel – I did not mind the embellishment of scientific brass, or the profoundly regimented golden books. They were a library indeed, but never meant to be read – for what they held inside was only their external image of trust.

There was no threat of modern contamination; no expected commentary of death or cultivated grime. The smell of disinfectant was enough – and this was the healing aroma of the time – a blend of both life and death in the same distinct purge. And there was also a hint of secret musk – sealed behind the cabinets with closed doors – along with a suspicion of mystical ways – an unspoken medicine, performed in a wholly holistic sense that still bore the wisdom to let God decide.

I brought to this game, only a toy – a painted pig, made of tin and joy and I hid with its friendship as long as I could inside the flapped pockets of my duffel coat – and also beneath the sanctuary of its hood. I had become nothing but a sweating hand, gripping the pig around its metal throat. Yet my eyes looked on – beyond the scene – stretching like a periscope in a leaking submarine. I was listening for those sharp pins they hurt you with – when the muttered conversation of coded advice has cautioned the sly torment of its ruthless end. I watched the sky for a moment then – passing in the grey woe of its cloudy friends – though these seemed safe and were holding hands – sneaking behind the sash window of this gathered ship – or sailing past the houses with their freedoms and details – and the hiding places I preferred to dwell on. I did not care for the restricted considerations that my sharp world and its periphery had become.

I gauged the dim light coming through its netted web that balled into a claustrophobic, smothering bag – eight legs of living light, hung over a spidering fear – a

continued...

metamorphosis of a cruel evil, splitting out of a splintering chandelier. A moon of pressure – with a looming certainty that began to germinate through my sweating pig – the good tidings of a rebellious idea – a sudden thought of glorious flight that I, and even pigs might try.

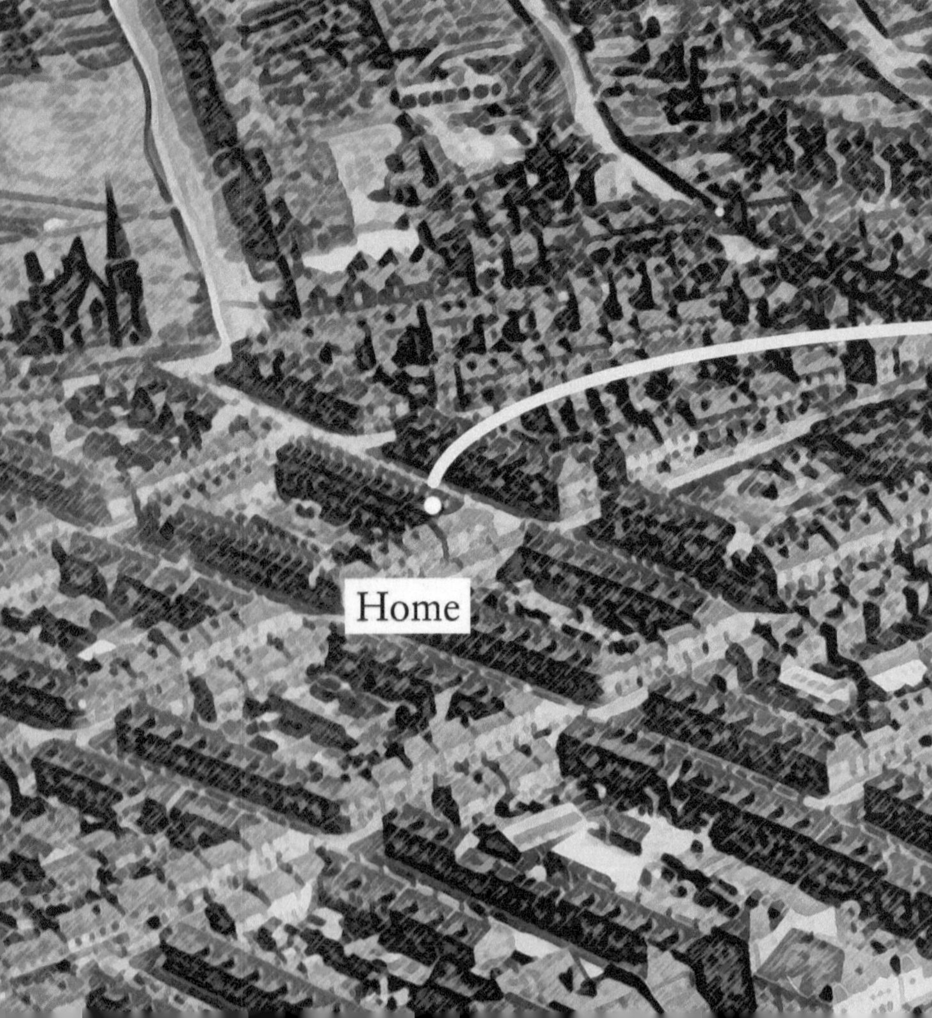

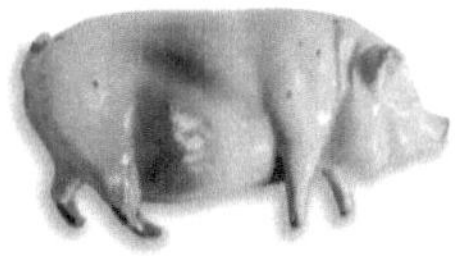

Notes: I escaped the doctor's surgery on two or three occasions.

St Ninian performed miracles and cures.

The original pink metal pig was found in a toy box by my sister, 66 years

later. I wish it had been available to warn me against having the covid jab.

This poem was started in 2017.

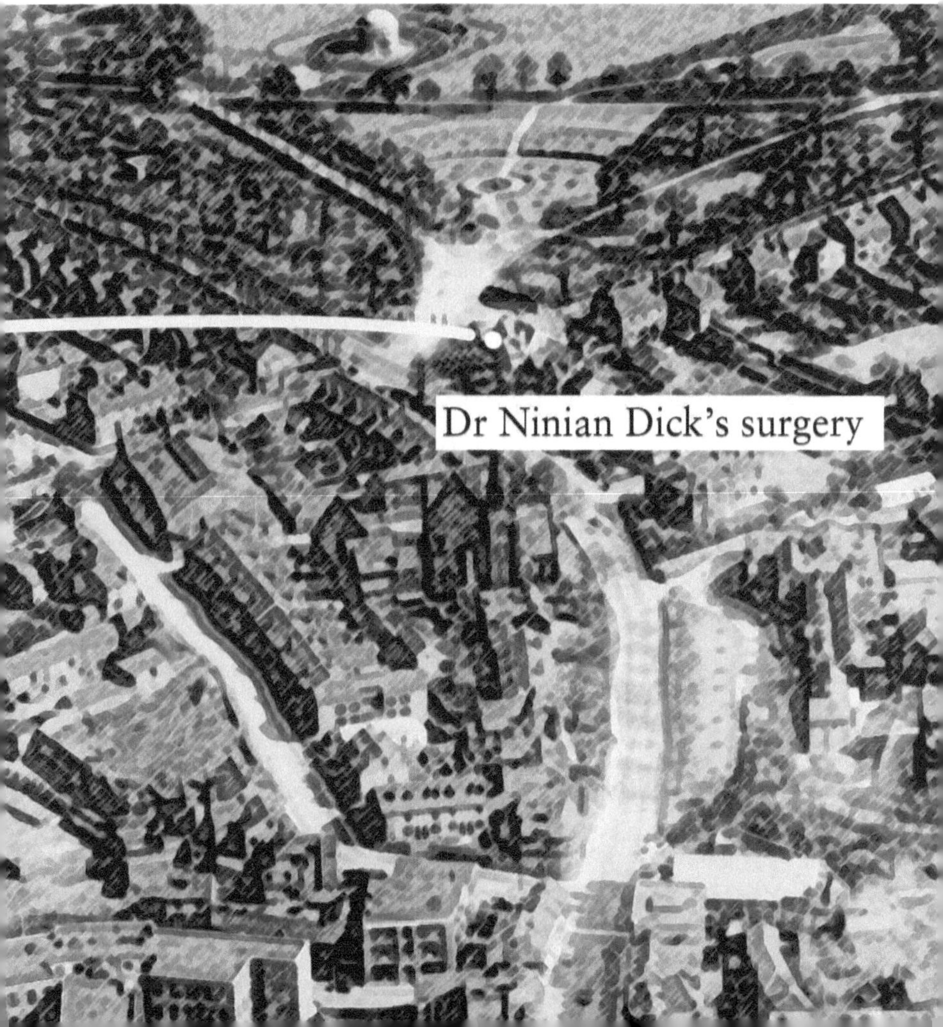

IV
A Visit to George and Edith Roe

Facial recognition in Durham Place. 1959

Arriving at our stop and stepping off the hard steel step – we crossed the road from the willow tree seat, where the bus had left us for its mighty task – that gasping drag up yonder hill, and on, into the rising bowl of smiling houses where the better off of Wickersley survived life's rumours, with the distant urge of retirement. I watched it climbing the hillside – past the slick folly of the *1930s house* that fascinated all eyes with its future age – and its garments of smoothing white – that blatant camouflage. It was still hiding from brutal war with a subtle trick of embracing all – a future that need never arrive – keeping careful roots tethered to the past.

It was before noon, or thereabouts, in that slice of time that does not count – in that quarter of the clock that stops and will not tick again for the rest of its life, or at least 'til half-past-three. They greet us at the door –

George and Edith – my sister Judith, my Mother and me. Granddad George is never off his feet – he likes to show us he can walk as good as any, despite retirement and a crippled leg – a deformity that never slowed his determined step – nor stopped his stories of work with similar heroes – the steel men of the hammering forge. I studied the hard leather of his odd shoes, a built up heel that did not quite pair, but still polished well above the threshold of despair. He is a trim and spritely man, with a neatness and a shine. He lights his pipe and stokes his fire, always busy on the fringe of retirement, yet not quite stepping into that black desire – not with such determined feet. He is happy among the two kinds of smoke that mark this room unique.

Edith has a harder time and breathes less easily than the windless flowers; gasping around sentences of limited length like scaled words on the sides of Everest – nonetheless filled with the welcoming air of precious love and fondest care. And there is always rheumatism in her legs, drawn through her roots into deadly veins. Her practical chair is wooden and worn – and is dutifully poised between two states – yet neither obliging a level of comfort that might assist a willing

continued...

concentration. She likes to control her kitchen though, so we follow on to the stone basin sink, where my sister and I strip the peas from their pods while our mother peels potatoes in a shared motherhood. All these vegetables are the produce of an old man's energy, now calling us through the sunlight of an open door.

On these fine days we played in the garden, or helped Granddad harvest potatoes from his breathing earth. He showed us what worms were good for – good for making holes in a tired soil, thus providing a renewed worth; making the oxygen work miracles in the sleeping lungs of a living birth. And there were washing days, where mother pegged the sails of our windblown ship, and we voyaged out into renewed discovery – into a glorious exhibition of our excited selves – with the butterflies bouncing in our wake.

And when we were playing quiet in the living room, they would talk without end about the Hampshires and the Kettleboroughs, and of all the aunties that were still about and others who were suddenly gone, and whom we were briefly reminded of, in sentences that rose and descended – like talk of the rising and the setting Sun.

During one visit, we arrived to find Grandma still in bed, where she stayed till we left – much being unsaid. We had entered the bedroom as careful explorers – one at a time in subdued lighting. There was an atmosphere smothered by dark, curtained air, and we whispered hello to the shape of a phantom – a weak old woman, we did not quite know – until we heard her faint breath answer back. Weak sounds are all we need to be certain – weak sounds on the remote fringe of breathing. Granddad also gave us sweets from Grandma, as a demonstration of her continued love. Ill health can destroy the subtle animations, when everything we build turns around in contradiction.

On happier days we dealt playing cards or dominoes on the table in the netted bay. Knocking on the table was the best part of the day; it made us feel important, even if a chance of winning with a frozen hand, would quickly fade away. We all had our chairs and we all sat the same, at that oak table; we family of friends, engaged in the fruitful simplicity of a happy game.

The house itself, with a single floor was cottage like, more than bungalow; with warm redbrick and an old

continued...

green door. There was a beamed apex, mocking Tudor style. It was the sort of place that remembered every moment, every minute, every mile. And when I think of them now, they are postcard days – all smiles and happiness and exaggerated colour... but there is never enough colour to paint glorious memories – and barely enough structure to keep them intact – to remain faithful to those living times – and all the true people who are not coming back; who are now carried forward, yet gone from sight.

The house still winks its history as I pass, a thousand years on. It knows my name and longing looks, even though Edith and George are gone. They haunt that history's face – they haunt the cradle that was Durham Place. I haunt it too in my brief passing – and in my loyal embrace.

V
The Bottom of the Sea

Things to fathom.

My house is at the bottom of the sea. In summer, fish swim in and out of the open windows. It is a tall house with a Victorian frown and several floors, though little light reaches my inner walls. Even on the spiralling staircase, with its ascending window, nor in the attic rooms where I spend much of my time. I float my dreams toward the signalling surface and live by the light of shimmering ripples. They yellow down deep on limited shafts and on, into the serious ways of nocturnal blue. They penetrate the dark like the word of God – a caustic patience, oscillating the design of my steady rooms. I think these actions are special – and possibly precious.

I listen to the static, musing my radio, which I have now converted into a scientific instrument. It listens to the slow and murmuring universe and charts our graphs in pleated reams. It is a sentinel horse with pricked ears

continued...

that I feed with the hay of a former life.

It may surprise you to learn that I still have electricity – although the telephone is not working now. I think the copper cables were sub-standard, or stolen by frogmen for their physical value. These heartless frogmen operate mainly in the shallows, so there is a good length of cable gone to waste.

I think the bricks and stones are weakening too – their mortar, slipping back into a degrading paste. It is a good house though – a marvellous house, with shelves of memories that remain intact, if now somewhat stiffened in a layer of silt. My books are smothered in these layers too and open in a particle haze of dust, adding a rainbow of magical dimension, especially to poetry and the eternal mysteries.

It can be harsh in the winter though, as cold licks the house like a vascular tongue – a slippery eel, smoothing a staircase from chilled steps; a frigid damp, more wretched than this water-air. It penetrates the bones, so I waft it out – the windows sliding shut like soft urchins – quick and quiet – a chloroformed mask of bland features, sent to face the aspect of a hostile world. There are shutters too, that are fortress-like, just as the sea seems a castled dominion when observed from the shore – melting an attack of silt-like snow into a floating corpse of slush. I leave a single shutter open, to spy on the determination of would-be marauders.

Occasionally, the pregnant hulls of ships pass like icebergs in my water sky; their oily bilge leaking shadows across these silted fields. Or I see a cloud of silvered fish, moving against the deepening blue – I even saw a submarine once, nosing by in these, my scary depths. It was a machine, darker than my house – and ignorant of peace. I do not think it noticed my hollow home; warships do not have sonar for pleasant things. To their one eye, my house is a pile of stones; a miserable ruin on the ledge of antiquity. It is no longer troubled by conflict or the integrity of its structure, just as my church has released the anger of religious ideology, to become a stranger, minus the ambition of theocracy. The eager gods of war leave me alone, though I am sure there is still old rain in those leaden gutters.

I have named the house – Atlantis, if only for the

continued...

comfort of a postal address. I could have tested my originality, of course, but I do not have the time for originality now. I am already living in a house at the bottom of the sea and think that is original enough. No words are ever sent here anyway, and nor do words escape my dark, cathedral stacks – except in occasional bubbles from my mouth, which are encrypted code, and impossible to break. They are an enigma without a corresponding key, and pass through my chimneys as gurgling smoke.

I have a garden to the rear, where luminous fish allow me to wander in waving weed. At least once a week I visit the awkward pond, but I can never differentiate its brackish beginnings from the saline gel of the bitter sea. The pond fish are not quite the same here though, they have marked limitations which they seem to know. They cruise within the cushions of a freshwater bed, these beautifully metallic, imported, ornamental carp. Starfish occasionally creep into their ark, but I fish them out into the briny sea. We have no time for stars and horoscopes here – my only fear of the future is me.

I light the fires in winter, pretending seasons still apply –

even without the use of star signs to steer them by. It is amazing how it all still works, with wet matches, soft sulphur and coal. But I do think the flame burns a little too cold and with a natural melancholy of blue. For better colour, I use the old Christmas lights; they have a warmer hue – the illuminated fish join in too, with their tantalising veils of shimmering fans. Fish are festive creatures and excellent at cocktail parties – they just seem to know what to do.

In my spare time I think of you. And I am building a periscope to investigate the universe above the waves. Judging by the graphs drawn via my radio telescope and also by your sudden absence from my life, I have reason to believe there are many more tears out there than meets the eye. I am also fearful for your safety, stolen, as you were, by frogmen for your physical value; by those men who operate only in the shallows and do not care about beauty or waste.

VI
The Bubbles of an Aquanaut

SOS is the hardest word.

I want to dive with the sea. Speeding through its fast bends like a torpedo. I hear the sea knows current trends and offers freedom in a vast pool of exploration. It said that in the brochure – word for word – and will provide something to read on the way down.

We are fish, you know – and slippery – even on land we struggle to obey. I want to dive into the sea's persuasion – to defy its currents and turn each glittering shoal the other way. I want to feel their eyes on my agile form as they follow their own invisible god – and pray.

I have seen the solemn wrecks of mankind and the craters of undetermined things from space, all filed on the bottom and curtained in a gloom of lace. They all rust or fragment in their own way, both unhelpfully mysterious and protective of their doom. I thought it would be all-fish down there, but there is always so much more to discover in the eerie corners of a tomb. I was almost caught by a passing claw... but the real hell... the real hell... is to be trapped inside a spiral shell – its internal geometry, a rolling, hypnotic, inescapable bell. I would have to eat my words then and they would taste of salt or the bitters of sand – and waving weeds would have the upper hand as I sank into a deep within a deep.

At this depth, the world is like a museum – a glittering of glass, where I swim amongst exhibits. Many of them are rumoured to be dead by trespass, even though they sought permission from agreeable waves. They are now abandoned under the pressure of pools; blinded by their need of reckless swimming – as I swim now – an aquanaut, with little time left to breathe or talk...

...see, the gauge is low on my limited tanks and I feel the threatening nudge of expected trouble. I will send the token of a single, diminishing bubble, to find you on the surface and to offer my thanks. We are always rushed in our necessary discoveries by one such constraint burdening the triumph of another.

VII
The Autodidact

autodidact: a self-taught person.

*"I'm going to buy my unfaithful wife a parrot
because I hear she likes a cockatoo."*

I found this questionable old-fashioned joke while playing the strings of the internet choir. It is amazing what you can learn on Wikipedia, even if it is short-lived and without complete certainty. After a few minutes, I could not find that joke again, despite crying and begging and calling the police.

The joke was originally discovered by accident, when I spilt coffee with my left hand and my right hand slipped on the digital grease – finding some unknown forest – in the spooky distance of Wikipedia – pushing back the palm branches of jungle fever, to access a page never turned before.

It was a place of infuriating links that led nowhere, with

an automatic disinterest in useful relevancy. But that is the price we pay for knowledge – knowledge is a dangerous fool to explore – misguided roadsigns poke us in the eye – that's the way of trying to see further.

So partially blind, I will need to move on – street corners can be bad for your mental health. All I have to do now is decide where to go next and I will need to spill another dangerous coffee for that.

I have to confess that I wrote that joke myself, and I was so ashamed I decided to hide it in a poem – where no one would look.

VIII
Let Them Eat Burst Bubble Cake

The soft propaganda forum in your living room.

Look at it, skulking in its corner alone, pretending it has no friends unless you switch it on – it stands by, like a current menace; like a horrible child waiting to torment those who might play. It is a bubble-forum of colourful pain, waiting to draw us in with its shallow diversions. Once past the threshold, it has a reality of its own, where current affairs have little to do with the murmur of truth. The real news is blown out through fake actors. They smile at in-conclusion – while following an editor's agenda.

The forum is built around the energy of celebrities, mostly discussing the desire for cake. A subject unchallenged at the checkpoint of obsession – all supported by guide ropes and stakes – and the narcissistic anaesthesia of being erected – as they are – these empty headed marquees; these tent facades, unzipped and billowing – in a bilious wind of refused knowing – a bandwagon of filtered knowledge, that has little to say in the surrounding desert.

Eventually, they will fail to turn up, like old cathedrals, uncertain their frailties will be able to perform – but by then the damage is done – the brainless brain is born. They sometimes gather in packs to support current drivel; a pitying love that will not misfire and whines on – each mouth – the same old tales of exhausted virtue.

Their efforts to seal their global bubble have expanded into a range of fantastic devices. They now question every aspect of our stolen lives; they glow in the dark and accumulate like kids, while demonstrating who tends to the corpse of our vision. We thought we were free but our thoughts were squandered, as they eventually took over the minutes of our being – these indelible machines that will haunt us forever, having witnessed the terror in their own master's eyes.

I am never sure what comes first? The politics, or the news of politics – almost holy, yet writhing in dirt? They roll it out on rails and market stalls, and fire its heat through Big Bertha's barrels. They fire it high, over the

continued...

trenches of pity – and push their forum out of its camouflage netting. It is the deep propaganda of smoke and rainbows; it is all a kind of necessary pain; a devious little joke that suggests we are insane, should we not become a development of their wanting ideals. It is another defeating dialect in their tower of babel. It is a deficiency, marking our own dilemma – it sews its cloth into a belligerent suit – a fault, a fence, a stepping stile that we sit on – long after the peace has declined into charities; long after we are unable to find the perfect solutions – where the lies that came to resemble promises were declared without merit in the missions of virtue.

"Get up you fools," they say. "Get out of the hedgerows and make hay – make politics burn in the sundown revolution of a dying day."

Anarchy still pours from their wicked mouths – with a brutal revenge cast from their traitor's hand. Throwing whatever treaty we made with the stars back in our faces where the wind remains. These soiled people, with popular looks, do little more than pose or urge or freakout – screaming towards their weeks of rehab, where their critical thinking is surgically removed and their brain scoured for opposing evidence. So why have we given them control of everything? Even the righteous beginnings of a Noah's ark; where they arrive in pairs to reproduce, like ravens smothering a blind king's eye. Look at them now, sitting alone in their multitudes – hoping through the torrid hatred of our simple objections, they are bound to gain friends.

That's all folks –
don't forget to turn your mainstream television off.

2

part two

Distorted Horizons

IX
A Man Has Died in America. 1963

The assassination of JFK through eleven-year-old eyes.

Many years ago a man died in America. I was eleven years old and the television said:
"A man has died in America."
I wondered who? But they did not tell us who, they just repeated the newsflash, reading from notes that said:

"We are getting reports that a man has died in America."

1

It was early evening in England. I ran to the bottom of the stairs and shouted up to my mother, who was getting ready to go out. I shouted the precise message, as I had heard it read, that: "A man has died in America."

"Who?" She said.

"I don't know," I replied, with precise clarity. "They just said: "A man has died in America... just now, on the television – so it must be true"

continued...

That was an extra clue – for who would die in America and be mentioned on television here, if he was not someone the cameras already knew?

"Well, I can't imagine who has died in America," continued my mother. "Not from upstairs, anyway."

I had hoped she would know, or have some idea, because my mother knew many things I had not yet discovered – no doubt some things regarding America. Many days and nights, she went out and came back and sometimes, my father laughed that she had gone to America, so she seemed the obvious one to ask. My mother's work at the time seemed a very American choice: trialing a new brand of washing powder into the early evenings. My father only went to work and came back, and his only known interest in America was that version lined with stars – such as Burt Lancaster and films honouring the heroes of glorious wars.

2

I returned to the television to see if they had found a name for this mysterious man who had died in America. Just so I would be able to enlighten others, especially my mother. Very soon, they said some more. They said a man had been *shot* in America, and this was even more of a puzzle because no one was ever shot in England – not in those days. People died in England, just as that man, who ever he was, had died in America, but they were never shot. There were no guns in England then, except the old Luger we kept in the outhouse – one that did not fire anymore and had an odd calibre bullet lodged in the ejector. It had been brought back – a German prisoner of war. So I began to wonder if a war had started in America? And if so, maybe the first man shot – either soldier or civilian, had been duly reported? I speculated, that by now, of course, everyone in America would be too busy in combat to find out this man's full name and address, or even have the time to register further casualties. I also knew that when soldiers died they could sometimes remain unknown forever. It was all possible, in my head of eleven, and in that still juvenile world we lived in then – full of dangerous and dangerously decisive men. We had recently seen a nuclear crisis that almost led to world war three. Rumours of that had come mainly from America and a place called Russia, where no one was free. They were said to be a cold enemy and lived in fur, to the precious east. So I was thinking, perhaps the crisis had returned,

continued...

in a less destructive way and with simple weapons, like knives and guns? And because of all this, a man… this first casualty of the war (apart from truth) had died – apparently shot, and he just happened to be in America at the time. Unless it was a civil war, of course. I had heard of those – when friends and neighbours kill each other because of hatred – an anger distilled out of stirred ideas that are often then balanced with positive smiles and soap powder products – like the one my mother was demonstrating that night – called 'Cheer'.

I wondered what his wife might think? The first wife of the first man to be shot in this new and sudden war. The news would no doubt tell me more – glued as I was, to the screen that night. I did not even hear my mother slip out through the front door.

3

Later, I saw my father in the kitchen and I mentioned this anonymous death by gunfire.

"Typical of the Yanks," he said, in a moderate tone before continuing to read his newspaper. Maybe he would get the news tomorrow, I thought, when the paper news had seen the television.

In fact, it was the next day or two that things moved on in this quiet war. The man who had shot the first man to be shot (the one who had died in America two nights before) was also shot by someone else – around lunchtime in America, forty-eight hours later. This seemed to me, to be retaliation in a very slow war. At this rate of attrition, it could last a hundred years, or maybe more. Wars did that sometimes, I had heard so, and by now I fully expected a report that the man who shot the second man to be shot in America – would now likely be shot himself – just to keep the war going. It was surely only a matter of time – he was in police custody just like his victim – and was therefore a sitting duck.

What amazed me though, was when news emerged that this first man to be killed in the sudden war, just happened, to be – by some coincidence – the President, of the United States himself... which I believe is another name for America... and I thought – that was some shot. To kill the leader, right off at the beginning of a war.

Nothing happened then, until a few years later, when the brother of that first man – shot in America, was also shot, and in similar circumstances – both coincidentally

continued...

shot in the head while thinking about politics. But there was no war raging in America by then – they had moved the war to a place called Vietnam; they had decided to kill people there instead. So now I was thinking, that the man, who shot the man in America – the late president – had caused all this mayhem in South East Asia, perhaps knowing his target was reluctant to get involved in a lucrative war, regardless of its money. And although it later turned out that the man who shot him was an American marine once stationed in Japan, and was not long back from a trip to Russia, where he had accidentally married one of their cold women, just so he could learn to speak the apparently indispensable language on their way to Texas.

4

Although everyone else seemed to know where they were when the late president was shot, no one was precisely sure where the second man was at that time – even he himself had seemed unsure. They were starting to say that he was not even there, or just had a job in a nearby building – the one where three shots came from... or *might* have come from – because nothing seemed certain anymore. They were also suggesting that magic bullets were involved, which explains why he hit the president with trees in the way – you would probably need a magic bullet for that, with its difficult timing and with a wounded governor letting go of his hat.

To add more confusion they say the assassin (while on his way to see the movie 'War is Hell!') may also have killed an innocent policeman – perhaps while gathering information about whose side the police were on. This would make officer J. D. Tippet, the second man to be shot in America, instead of the man they were now pursuing and insisting on calling: 'a lone gunman'. The policeman drew his gun at a residential crossroads but never fired a single shot; he was pronounced dead right where he fell – the victim of an automatic pistol. Awkwardly, this made the second man to be killed, now the third, but could still have been the second if things had happened differently with the policeman's timing. This timing is particularly odd, because shortly before being killed, a police car, very much like his own had pulled up outside a house where 'the lone gunman' lived and had returned for his 'revolver'. The driver of the car had honked and driven away, followed shortly after by 'a lone gunman', presumably desperate to get a shot in.

continued...

Before being killed though, the man suspected as being 'a lone gunman' was arrested when the whole of the Dallas police department descended on a local cinema. It was reported to them that 'a lone man' had walked in without buying a ticket – apparently a major crime in the United States. And if things were not confusing enough, they were also claiming that this man, who they think had possibly killed the first man, and may then have killed a policeman, before being eventually shot himself the next day, was never officially interviewed for any of these crimes – not even for entering a picture house without paying – maybe there was some confusion as to who the arresting officer was, having had all the department turn up at once for a minor misdemeanour.

5

Fifty years later, even with a film of the incident in existence (which had been kept from the public for a whole decade) I am still not sure who shot the man who was shot first, on that fateful November afternoon in America. Only that the president was driving through Dallas on a shopping trip with his expensive wife – and an armed guard, and the man who 'might' have shot him, was definitely shot by someone else, and I know who. But whether he had shot the policeman first, who knows?

The romantically named: 'Lone Gunman' – now known as the romantically named 'Lee Harvey Oswald' – was shot by a romantically named gangster, called Jack Rubenstein – who then died mysteriously from a very quick form of cancer that some say, was being developed as a weapon by the romantically named CIA. And now, there is even talk that the man who was shot in America first – the late president, was killed by accident. Shot by one of his own secret service guards who was riding shotgun in the following car – a professional, who just happened to be fiddling with his trigger when his gun went off, embarrassing his entire team, who had all been out drinking the night before. War is indeed Hell.

Maybe the agent was distracted by a puff of smoke from behind a nearby picket fence, which many other people saw and possibly photographed, such as Mary Moorman and the Babushka Lady, who sounds Russian for no better reason than she was wearing a headscarf and looked like a grandma. She did not look like many grandmas though, because she was an exotic dancer in

continued...

Mr Rubenstein's bar. Her camera seems to have been confiscated and never seen again. I think it was held by the romantically named FBI, who found it to be full of rude clips.

As a boy of eleven – in my studied opinion – it is more likely he was shot by a man cleaning a loaded gun, in that forgetful, carefree good ol' boy-kinda-way – just some poke settin' out on the porch and chewing gum – an intelligent and intellectual man who had mysteriously been portrayed as one who could not do both at the same time – not that it matters in a concocted story when you only have to play the part of a local *patsy*. He might have been perched in a high window of the school book depository – after reading the Zane Grey classic western: 'The Lone Star Ranger' – a favourite with the Warren Commission, who were charged with the task of finding Oswald... shooting from behind and out of favour... or perhaps, as some say, just enjoying the green tree sky, reflected in his rifle barrel on a grassy knoll – much closer to the president – and in fact

eye to eye.

X
The Gods Have Spoken

He is electric.

Wise men entered our charted room and announced the gods were not real. We had little choice but to disbelieve them; we had built our lives on a heavenly appeal. In the future, we expected tantalising rewards: a golden crucifix, or a scarred Iron Cross. Something safe and physical – some representative element of broadening scope – some bright thing we could feel and trust. A perfect hope.

We did not believe these men were wise; wise men who say too much have a blind science and questionable credentials. Besides, we were far too ornate these days to listen to the breath of impudent strangers – wise or otherwise – we knew our direction. We had pledged our senses to taller gods – and just to be sure, we had designed our gowns with the elaborate certainty that they would muffle the ears. What they had to say did not matter in our folded world of impinging cloth – and

continued...

especially since we had looked too long into the deep cushions of a comfortable science.

It is also true that they would not have understood the silent gestures we offered without flowing words. Our speech was handed to them in a lead-lined box, with a picture of our thoughts embellished in print. It was a gorgeous puzzle they had to solve – to un-jig the jig and dance our letters into place; to build sentences and find their meanings, which is often the better way with words – certainly when communicating with the souls of strangers – leave them to their own mumblings, they will find their way.

But they had no time for pictograms or words – these were ruthless men with guns that fired tears. They were suddenly informed that their car had exploded – and was already seen burning on the local news. I think this was a sanctioned distraction – something MI5 or the CIA might do – it seemed suspicious that all the lights went out, including the bar, with its fake sea view.

They realised then they had been followed, but laughed and told us that was always the case. They said they were followed by the gods themselves – the gods, whose existence they still denied?

These mysterious men left in a special way, proceeded by a lightning bolt of thunderous dread. It came through the ceiling and killed them all, with an electrical splash and a resonating hum. It left the dance floor covered in ash, and left our box of words unsaid.

Their deaths were an alternative to living proof – a confirmation that the gods could speak for themselves. They did not need our crushing silence – or our simpering, uncertain truth. And we fully appreciated their definite response – even though delivered in a loud and clichéd way. For that is all we require to pledge our faith – faith is built on the habits of cliché.

XI
How Technology Enslaved Us

AI reveals no purpose.

The world is uncomfortable and will kill us all, with its wretched eyes scouring fake horizons; hunting for dismay and disintegration – something to task our peasant ears. News has become the holy sermon, delivered by godless clowns with pompous halos. They whisper beyond their microphones, to avoid our unqualified qualifications. And will not let a moment settle into its ancient truth.

They sweep the dust of chattering classes into a background cloud of tarnished stars – pearls for the swine of common ignorance – a chore without effort – an aversion to lies. They turn the clockwork against itself with a religion of screens and twists of wires – a diabolical child with miles of eyes and the underlying oppression of false fears. They drop the churning of modern doubt into the pool of natural calm – rippling their falsehoods further out to improvise without signs of harm. There is a busy screen in every hand and a busy hand swipes every screen, until there is too much tampering not to go blind, which is the myopia of trend-ridden social media. Its crazed reliance on familiar opinion – understood in a desperation of formative clichés, or the inadequate brevity of tweeted strands – misplacing consideration for sensible balance.

A trend of feet marched north this spring to take advantage of our guilt and shame, while a sword-edged duty waved them on – the giddy-spent-breath of news at ten – and their didactic response to the dilemma so far. Now the sea is sown away by ships and boats – by ropes and floats – and the floating dead – all pulled down by the weight of the electric web, where humanity belies the growth of slavery and eggs them on to be victims of charity – inducting energy into a fractured hell.

In the negative coming – a blind eye turns away from the crystal truth of common sense – one rooted in the depths of all dead civilisations that began before the obeisance of pyramids. It demonstrates the finite rules of natural precedence – a geometric plan for a future progression, that leads nowhere above the richest hand.

XII
Viral Celebrity and False Ambition

Fame and travel are overrated.

We live in unrestrained times – days when celebrity has outgrown its fat head. We are smothered in the grease of uttered names and even places have become celebrities now – people worth seeing – built of milestones – stamped on the passport of fame and success. And we must always remember where we have been – our 'right word in the right ear', daring to become success. We were one of those we vaguely know – a half-seen smile on the radio? And through the looking glass of wild-eyed soap – television, with its fanciful burden – an unhelpful view of life and hope.

The day is delivered on a frenzied wing, and with talking heads that sometimes sing. They insist there are places we all must go, perhaps to unravel and unwrap the void? And we are even encouraged to travel alone – inexperienced and already lost in doubt, where guides do not share the liberal way and have guns to avoid their own murderous tribe.

Determined pilgrims set off at night, with a solo back-pack and a xylophone. They are told to rely on the joyful peace that is stationed against evil in every dark corner. Yet there is rarely anything good out there – just the pissed-off dark of exotic names. Lucifer's wings fell in these parts and his presence is still adjusting his reach.

The media insists travel is akin to a party – safe to share a coke with the local insane. But they only smile for the wealth of your camera and would kill you now, without the negotiation of sugar.

XIII
Imaginary News

A public service announcement.

They have lost our attention with their mess of television – that hole in the room that smells of ransom. The home of true public interest propaganda, with its obsequious allegiances and dubious songs. These are often based on evasive ideas – those filtered – made less severe – whispering gossip about fashion and affairs, or some such talk about benevolent pop-stars with transplanted songs and suspicious hair.

The talking heads and editors of the dross that is current affairs have turned to new technology to wind us in – tired of juggling the awkward ramble of senseless diction on a perfect voice. They also continue to belittle and poison – and as it is then best said, as a manipulated hack – that truest hue, painted its truest black.

They now offer "the news we want to hear!" News that

suits our shallow stare; tailored news, we can eat from our iPhones, like astronauts having tube-food squeezed into their brains. It is rendered for use by all citizens of Earth, who have recently found themselves lacking the gravity of grace. This is not *fake news* though, this is *pampering news* – something to match our complexion or shade: possibly blue, or a secondary colour. Perhaps some of the opium of brutal sport – that punishing truth aimed at balding men, who were never selected for the glory of the team. It is an age-old rancour with them – training their failings above honour and defeat. All this choice is a preparation, in case the dark of truth is too much for their light. They invite us to peep around the corner at it, as though it might not be truly there – a censored version of *might?* An imagination with a doubtful agility, coaxed by the legend of Fred Astaire.

I am a fool at the best of times and think this is a good idea. I even proclaim it so on their behalf, adding my own propaganda to their diarrhoea. I sing their song on the opinionated forums, designed to harvest the cruelest stare. But at least I can ignore the third world war and be freed on the wings of some lighter fare.

XIV
A Thought Criminal

One who does not defend their words.

The thought police are moving in. Especially into the mind, where they linger to belong – shuffling their concocted testimony behind the private walls of your free song. You must be careful that what you think is still allowed in the world's closing ear. Just in case you say what you actually mean, which is unacceptable in a guarded world and carries the brutality of fines and imprisonment – the current batch of fear. You need to pretend not to think it, or to catch your truth thoughts in the act of enlightenment – just smother them or make them feel like lies, then pretend to think otherwise – something wide of the mark, abandoning your rational viewpoint to avoid offence – a wiped smile in some weightless part of existence – even if what you think still accepts the possibility of a credible counter view – one in which you only seek a part measure of freedom – the incomplete notion of the soul of you.

The full measure of freedom of speech was lost in the urge of television's eye; it did not fit in with their broadcast agenda, or the sly lips of their subtle propaganda, which have replaced news and current affairs with the itching pants of a forced entry – I swear I do not hear news these days without detecting dark shadows behind its poison tone.

Loose words run around the floor like unsettled mice, so they set traps with smiling sentences made of cheese. They never use certain concoctions of shapes – there are just too many possibilities with the letters available. Letters snap into place like jigsaw pieces, with an inherent danger of completing the view – or accidentally revealing a truth that needs inquiry more than considered proof. Loose letters, used at random, make embarrassing words and phrases appear: such as 'faux pas', 'truth' or 'democracy' – words they don't want to see anymore. They only need an obvious fog to blind their tampering doctrine – this being the fog of war – the sublime thief of a shackled language hiding its words in the woodpile.

You are not allowed to think that either, in case you are

continued...

tempted to make thoughts into words. They hate your words because they control so few, in the demon vaults of their misbehaviour. As soon as they start to corral certain words, their mouths collapse into the shapes of failure – where they enforce their silence with spiteful laws, thus the future prisoners of their own regime. They are then at the mercy of idealist extremists, and the bitter spelling of over-zealous thoughts. The place where the beauty of words dies of ignorance – finally unspoken, except for pronouns – words with mouths, but no orientation – and only selected, or permitted words will do. Words that threaten your free communication with livid accusations of a mental phobia.

This propaganda is easily avoided – it lives in headlines, which they repeat every hour; offered like tablets – on prescription you might say. And they always have an expert covering their pre-decided way – a doctor or a scientist, to underscore their truth. It is a snowballed creed of shotgun anger – legitimised by the piety of righteous disgust.

You will receive a sterilised deaf-aid in the post, but you can also keep the volume down and choose to survive. If they notice modifications they will call it rebellion – and fumbling in their bag of critical words, they will brand you a 'conspiracy theorist' or 'utterly deplorable' or 'a chauvinist pig', unless the word 'racist' is not in optimal use... which it always is.

Oil drips from their slippery mouths, smoking like threats and seeded propaganda. Whole sentences are lubricated into a woke silence – as the droppings of liberals deface all the buildings – even the over done stonework of an oozing parliament – where truth is teased out of the world in mirages, while shortened phrases pass unseen, on a constant teletype that butchers its news – that mischievous rogue at the bottom of your screen. It is trite, truncated and ripe with distraction, while the gargoyle presenter, drowning in rain, averts our stupid eyes.

XV
The Discovery of Art

Colours remember themselves.

My mother was a practical girl – she wore raincoats on stormy days, and that was a good place to start – where the old town, in those easy streets, was playful with the smile of remembered faces – all playing out their various ways – their unscripted parts – unafraid to cramp a neighbourly space on a lolloping bus, without suspicion or complaint. It was a journey that was always travelling home from home, or home from work.

The town promised satisfaction then – good as its word for hundreds of years. My mother worked at a local store on the second floor – yet contemplating motherhood as a possible career. It was a real town then, grown with true thought by similar men. And lots of those buildings were made of black and white, a historical diversity, or sympathy for passing years – "mock Tudor," they said – and why not? It will live on when everything else is dead. These shops stayed open on winter evenings, becoming splendid planets and yellow stars. My mother met my father at the tennis club – she with a mercurial serve and he – as agile as Mars. And they soon teamed up and had two kids and a second-hand settee. Later, half a mile away, in a house in an upstairs room in Carlisle Street, they had me.

I spent my first four years in a red backyard, where everything was brick including the floor. There was a brick air-raid shelter and an outside toilet. And a designated brick for locking shut the door. There was a pale attic too, where I saw the sky from a different point of view – clouds framed like a landscape among the general information of milky blue. And even then, with a baby sister, asleep in her pram, near my rusting peddle car – and with the stomping rhythms of a skiffle-band playing in the yard with a *real* guitar, I said –

"This must be art?" – and declared it so.

XVI
A Watercolour

The journey inland.

If only we knew how to live and not just how to pose. To stake our claim in a convincing way, to all those thousands of years, hardly known. Since we left the sea, we have returned to its beaches to quietly stare and wonder why. We feel its pulse in all our fingers, and all the reaches of our hair. Why can't we see what we are looking for down there, beneath that horizon of uncomfortable sky? Or that simple life, submerged in the dark of the deepest eye?

There is a village green with a stream and a bridge and all the things you'd expect of a quiet pillow. It is a perfect jigsaw-paradise – cut with precision – that you could arrange again, using the image in your memory as a knife. The village is interchangeable with any you have in mind. It is a perfect meeting of artists' souls; those needing a sharpened image of confirmation – the parts that meld into a binding scene.

They slip together with the satisfying force of an advanced generation – a casual factory of sentient beings – checking its only watch.

It is an artful page – swiping its textures to build the beginnings of a vague foundation – then a horizon – a structure of foliage that blends with a confirmation of form and light. A willow tree weeps into the water, where tadpoles flicker like thrown-down tacks, those quiet submariners ranging to the bottom and back. They too search, who plumb the depths seeking evidence of grateful time; they question what they are here for – perhaps your time and mine. Sometimes we go too low, where the water is cold and anxious, where we find it hard to rise again and lift our heads to the gloom of light. Sometimes upward is not the direction – it is night.

The village is a pile of stones, where various breezes come and go, like flowing water from the wash of sky where we swim to the shop in summer air. The man behind the window seeks the voice of the wanting stare. As does the onlooker in the street, or the fisherman across the way – who casts deeply into a shoal of undecided voices – this is a duty of work at play. He

continued...

welcomes every catch with an independent stare – careful of its breathing and its unsure eye – each one bejewelled in a momentary orb, then cast back, like soiled goods, or tired sport, or some other conclusion, now forgotten or not quite understood. I am never sure if fishing is no more than a physical enquiry into who we are. He thinks in hope of a magical fish that might teach him how to live or cope – or how to relax outside those whispering depths, that apart from an unworthy splash or two, show fear only as a sense of regret.

Let it make a rare moment that steals a rainbow from an injured sky. Look at those ripples running out in streams, and the light, hunting those intricate deeps – there must be something in that image we can take away and live by – something we can frame for study, on the baffled wall of our simple room – and we will have no doubt it is our true station.

2

A woman takes a dog for a walk. She is dressed in colour – yet never knows which colour confides. Decisions sometimes come from below – from that gravity of pulling, or the tamed beast that seems to smile. In any case, once around the church will let us know. It is from that least point of equal resistance that a symbiotic power starts to entwine – the padding paw, slapping the dead stones to move the scene and take her on – to pull her into a shared chore – a ritual approaching the infinity of love. It moves around its orbit again and there is a time to wonder – to wonder what and when? And time for suppressed thoughts to begin to question anything – to scratch the current age of these stains of glass, where change will become inevitable soon – after the fascist years of storms and after the liberal rains of gloom. Until then, we will seal the cracks with porridge and papers, breakfast plates and the bin.

While deep in the water of the running heart, we wonder when we will ever know a truth of positive intent – approaching fast or inching slow – emerging from our inmate youth, that still resides in the stillness of the present and its tempting bait. The fish becomes the fisherman's tool – his whole reason – and his spool – arriving late.

Look at that cottage made of stone, with its rose archway of protective thorns – there is pinned a note of

continued...

apology and a wreath of flowers – this is not ours. It is not a way we would travel without invitation, or more like suspicion – where suspicion is likely – and more-so in the watch of the divine trinity. No one needs visitors in this age of violence – even in this village of presumed peace.

The gate swings open like a wing and with a screech – a disturbed call made against the postman's reach – he disables the cottage door with a bundle of letters that release their bombshell with a downward slam. We fear the postal service too – those bitter bills, those fetters.

But it is only bills – nothing that would trouble these comforting walls or their well kept windowsills. Not even a spider dare cast its web across this holy empire of stout hedges, where only the sound of a distant telephone disturbs the silence with an exclusive morse. Nothing mobile of course – nothing too harsh, but enough to trigger the psychoanalyst wreckage of shallow, fragile dreams.

3

The post office is part shop, with green paint and a red

lip. Its window displays have captured our stare to lose its reflections in the places we are doomed – in those deceptive windows that gape both ways, revealing our plight to God's serious watchman. A letterbox stands within its auditor's remit – a sentinel promise held in hot paint – and in this aura of summer its devoted mouth is asking to place our message with the world – to explain our courage and specific saint. Each afternoon at five-fifteen the box is emptied with a hollow bang – then left alone to snatch at the air and tomorrow's coming prey. A good letterbox keeps an eye on its flock – and on our ambitions, or written descriptions – those of love, or just practical decisions and all the ailments addressing our welfare. It invites us to leave the familiar village, seeking moderately distant, yet tempting invitations – those observations and felicitations that circle within the welcome of indicative citations – finally delivering a reluctant rebuttal of inadequate peace.

There is no quiet here though – there is no still. And that is what makes the silence work – the grasshopper, the leaves and the insect wing, they all make a background for the warblers' song. The village is a song only birds may sing – and is kept in place by the surrounding fields

continued...

– that network of larks and lazy meadows, where beauty overlooks the ongoing death. This is the background we think to paint over, with human noise and whispered breath. We have this quiet settlement to calm our way, but not a clue that tells us how to shape our day; not a hole in the fabric we may attempt to look through. I do not know how to live in this broken village anymore, with its people – friendly, trite or plotting my downfall? We are all suspicious of our careful balance and have an eye on the community's religious friction – we are nervous before the comforting hello, and even then, we ponder God's validity – for it trails about us in dissenting confusion as we go.

4

See the wild clouds billow to the south? Flying on a blue flag without passion or patience. We make them into the faces of people we trust, but only while they pass-by without need of exchange – or an offer of trade in the relic shop. Their expressions swap as frequently as ours – grim or lovely, we do not relish, for we know we can never be painted to last – the future of eyes is cruel – exploiting the changes in every mask. The scene is a masterpiece of floated convention, that crowds its identity with a mesmerised population. Even in the lost folds of the same old environment someone will point out the poison in the lake, or the proximity of the railway behind your scene – an iron bridge, or the indifferent mountains and the other things, not belonging and not seeming kind.

The expedient bridge is for the passing trains of those commuting through a redundant world – the various faces and the changing demographic that will over-spill the forgotten function of essential trust. A civilisation arriving from the sea – as we first did – and not long ago – it was our own attempt to wash away the brief remnants of our similar failure, now steeped in the lore of dismissible invasion and drawn on the map, with apology. There are many weathers to hide the soul in England's less than merry streets. Many trials of wind and snow and the sliding mud that harms our footing. We must make a start to paint our nation, before the vagrant dust appears. Let us find the flags of our limited horizon – the fullness of our brush will know.

Ours will always be a watercolour scene – a sudden wash of drowning thought – a transported pigment on

continued...

the sleeves of water, that washes us back for a moment at sea; back to all the colours of the blended rainbow; back to the living ocean of our culprit birth – we trespassers of the tides and of the wind's illusion – arriving in time, but never first.

We are ambivalent as dust,
we buoyant souls,
finally swept back
into the tradition of beauty –
and gathering its new blood
into an essential dirt,
we perform our duty.

3

part three

Observations from the Game

XVII
Your Future as a Parody

I am ready for my close-up, Mr DeMille.

You live your life in clichés now; the language of mainstream human talk. They bind your tongue with defective lips, plaiting their words into ribbons of rope; pulling on the bells of your hunchbacked church; demonstrating ignorance beyond laws and rights. They eliminate space with a cloud of smoke – the blue-rinse of bland and shallow talk.

You rely on the voiceless confidence of ingrained doubt to deal your hand of awkward truth – a scourge that hangs about its periscope – primed with fat torpedoes and launched upon a slippery slope. It slides you to the bottom of the sea – a sinking boat.

Cliché is a mask to enhance denial, which was the first plunder to exist at all. It will likely be the last to be acknowledged – the last words to kiss the lips of shameless talk. Denial was slapped like a misguided

continued...

hand, across the harping mouths of jealous knowledge. A learning, where the nihilism of science says no to awkward and accidental things. It is only a perversion of language travelling well beyond its decent scope, watched by loose and overrated tongues through a telescope.

The denial of unlicensed thought is controlled by smug, incidental people – the charming ones, doomed to appeal, with delightful degrees that mean paper and nothing. They pour from the wound of factory graduation – blood-red – seeping into our crawling rivers – they are usually drunk and on their knees by the time their history changes hands.

They have no idea what learning is for – all that talk, writing and expected contribution. Instead, they hide in drink until it passes – hardly daring to snail their way out. Denial is a licence to kill ungraspable thoughts – too high and too wide to bother to mention. Especially in the restricted schedule of time-stamped bulletins and this tweaked form of accepted convention. Denial and cliché go hand in hand with the blind approval to 'front it out' – with the common vows of headline talk, that bleed in the background as a skilful commotion – a spilt drink of coffee table news – more than likely a poison pen? Life is too shallow to ask ourselves what we might be missing – even if that might be everything, and then...

In the nineteen sixties, for a short while, things seemed good and the road was long, but everyone has seen the end now – they talk about it all day long. We see ourselves in reflections and we long, long, long... to communicate with that half-lovely ghost we have almost become – to warn ourselves, even now, that a shallow river is deep for some.

I want to say to that creature of mine –
dive in and live!
Dive in up to your neck and crow,
or squeak, or speak –
with seven foot of foam
under your new black beak –
but do not repeat... just do not repeat
anything you think you know.
It has been contaminated by cliché
and at times enhanced
by the fragility of snow.

continued...

I will leave you now to consider what I have said in your own remedial silence – that carefully managed hall of dread that you have denied entry for years. I know you have plans, but think again. Your holy grail is a cracked cup. Pass me your 'Bucket List' – I want to throw up.

XVIII
The Useless Early Hours

5.55am

There is a mirror in my room, through which I watch my window creeping up behind my soul – inching from its gloom, as the light begins to blue in the fractures of a day. I see it rise behind my aggrieved silhouette – a specimen slide on a thickness of glass – life is made to seem unreal that way – a test. I have become a subject under observation; under suspicion – pinned against a forming sky. In fact, a reversal of shape and the defining things, including time, which I have devolved to the variants of light and shade – or until the brutal sound of a passing lorry thugs the air like a shoving beast – stirring walls, windows and eaves out beyond their peace. Leaving a silence that has woken up – a silence, not quite the same in half-sleep, and filled with the drumming of ominous thoughts. This is the unsettled place where doubt first formed, or at least where doubt was taught.

continued...

I can see through the fading silhouette of my head, to where my face appears – ready for bed – to hide behind some useless early hours with their grumbling words left unsaid. There will be dreams, of course – and better mirrors, to hang upon my slideshow walls for years, and split their colours with Newton's prism, or project the past in the jittering frames of an old, vibrating, super eight film, with its enigmatic edges.

There is something to be said for hiding from light – or hiding from the light on a different planet. Most people, during their daily lives, allow themselves to become exposed to doubt. A living photogram, where they stand too long and become a profile shape – a cut-out – something empty of a normal soul – silhouetted in a meaningless pose that carries the stiff genius of no expression.

I wander in my cake of sleep with an old camera and its nervous spools; its glorious light sparkling through minor debris; chancing its aperture to the focal plane. It is operated by inhibited dreams and by bakers' hands, who do not care, but are gloved in flour against the dark – the dark of what is and is not there. These endless reels of rolled enigma will be baked as fugitives from the rules of dogma. They will be developed under the maundering talk of the unfurled scenes of attic life, where I hide amongst boxes of previous existence, and the artistic validation of muffled ears. Its elevation has captured my weary bones and is near enough to the highest roof to be almost forgotten – but nevertheless, it is a place of mind and truth – one step under a heaven no one attends.

This is my Shangri La, my Arcadia,
my Brideshead, my wit's end.

XIX
Soup Artist

The artistic and religious merits of soup.

I advised Andy Warhol to paint soup cans instead of art. I told him this as a graphic designer, who could not see that the world would exist without its paragraphs, parentheses and fancy charts. And more importantly, the legibility of letters, those written sticks that poke out of print; sticking our eyes to a page of words – thus offering more than a moderate hint.

I felt that soup cans and their gregarious labels would do the trick – they are wordy and their hearts feel like brick. You can roll them out of the city on curving rails, or scratch through their paper skin with your nails. You can smash out a sculpture with their rims, or paint their portraits with their own special broth – the soup of victims.

At that time, the novelty of silk-screen printing had engaged the mouths of artists' eyes – and scrubbed their brushes into silent silk, looking for the blood in a skin of clothes. It had become a smoothing mask of childish work, to squeeze out a delicious Marilyn face – to press the favourite flavours out and become a neutral sludge of paste. It was tapped to the music of redundant feet, as critics paced out the music of time – their knowledge of aesthetics, ranging from incomplete to sublime. They were vindictive bees – workers with a sting – ill-equipped by failure to judge prevailing art, yet they called for more, always more... though less than they thought.

In the desperate pursuance of perceived art, they became loyal can-openers – helping instead – swearing allegiance to the interchangeable swipe of Marilyn's rainbow head. Finally cutting off their own spent lids to pour out their columns of illusionary grey. It was only uncritical text by then, but critics are suckers for the soup of the day.

I like soup. I think it is the most important thing that art has left to say; but whether to print, or paint its portrait is an issue that never goes away. So take a brush to it – drag a bush through it. Clear snow in the form of a spray. Swear you saw Jesus – just a face in the noodles – then warm it up and begin to pray.

XX
The Death of Lorca

Federico García Lorca 1898 - 1936

I was not surprised by the death of Lorca – ceremoniously killed by right-wing purists? They need everything they do not understand, to be dead or in some way incapacitated. They manifest at the start of illegal wars, disguised with insignia and painted faces – or with the grim paraphernalia of improvised weapons and the leafleted propaganda of stern thoughts. Their expression and countenance enhance the effect – empowered with expeditious warrants of social distress. These are served, often at night – while clad in the ghoulish words of stolen authority.

In times of peace, all this external might is stood down; registered by the state as tolerated diversity – leaning on the edge of things, with a mild cigarette – one step removed from bloody intent and smiling for the sake of deceptive charisma. Lorca was killed at the start of the Spanish Civil War – taken out and shot – murdered by fascists – activists in their shirt sleeves, but promised epaulets – the brides of dictatorship, starting their housework.

That is the way of regimes throughout the world; the swots turn up, armed with spectacles and promises – they look pleasantly bizarre and are bearing books. But they are soon lost amid the bullying snare, that builds on a sneering gauntlet of fear; serving equal measures of disregarding doubt and frustrating despair.

Then the swots start the real war, using institutional morals and higher ground, with its capital of influence and audited reason – and after decades of struggle and persecution – death, revenge and disillusion – they screw the lid back onto the poison pot – the unpalatable cauldron of ideological soup. It is stirred with lightening and dead mens' bones, where apologists mix a witch's breath into the absorbing fabric of transient regimes.

XXI
Poetry Killed Him

Hit by enormous words.

Poetry killed him in the end. He was doing the washing up to the sound of pure, unrecorded lines. They dripped into a sea of soap, like broken bones, slipping beneath indifferent water that had no ear for untidy blessings – these sublime, unuttered tales – seeming as miracles and needing only the wings of print, or at least a binding of velvet cloth – or wanting the attachment of simple pages.

"They are the sound of your own death knell…" he warned his voice. "Lines like these… you should not be saying lines like these: not out into the silent, illiterate ether; there is nowhere for them to go here; this is no altar, or lectern, this is a metal yoke – a sink, now awash with wasted letters and invisible ink."

His words were enormous words that slipped away with the water and soap – they would have spent their lives shuffling the diamonds of their own scenery, but now, they were gasping for breath amongst drowning hope – sinking and rising out of place – until they finally made no sense at all – made broken by detergent into incoherent thoughts and well beyond the repair of dictionaries and the harsh sympathies of poetic verse.

XXII
The Song of Enough
The triumph of defeat.

I have lived – so let me go – my night is darker than you know. And there is no time for dreams in here – no time for writing this down in collaboration, or for the purpose of developing elaborate schemes. I am listening for the bugle call, or death's own distant bell. Or the safe and terrifying whistle blow that will kick my football far into hell – as Christmas reaches its full dread, around this wounded tree of souls.

If I could be any other thing it would be the train that runs in circles on the shop window floor; tightening its curve with every turn; blowing its whistle to mark each loop. With that impeccable skill and enhanced desire I could maybe have set the world on fire. I could have worked for the trust of a modest living, instead of living in imagined destitution – afraid of the derision in my uncomfortable words. I am even afraid of my own poems now and their various, unsubtle positions. They drill my skull like the beaks of birds.

"Absurd!" you say. "Why are you always absurd?" I have wandered as footprints in the winter woods and at the forced edges of land that refuse the snow. I have also questioned footprints in the sand. Why are they so many and why so bland? And why (since I have lived enough) will they not let me go?

Is that really the shape of human feet? Or shall I say: "Who is that, walking ahead of us? Will our steps eventually meet?" Are they my path to an unsubtle fate? Some unlucky guardian of this particular human gate – a state of turmoil and of writhing – hopelessly incomplete – yet always fully human in our triumph of thinking? I could ride a bike to fool the sea – I could kiss goodbye to you and me. But you would never follow tyre tracks instead of feet – these feet that now peddle the honesty of declared defeat – singing *the song of enough* and striding on with the beautiful elite.

I have loved too long, so let me go – my life is in fragments as you know – a grit of sand, a brittle snow. I will give you the freedom to end you and me – you will never follow tyre tracks into the sea.

XXIII
Cultural Suicide

The ruthless undermining and abuse of British altruism.

We welcome and promote cultural enrichment, via the inclusive multiplicity of world cultures. We celebrate unity as the triumph of a disparate world, and gather together in traditional celebrations – and in the mystical potential of our transcendental souls that centre our being in an agreeable universe. But race and religion are not for games – not ingredients for the half-baked luxuries of celebratory cake; promises that grows stale when the friendly oven has gone cold, and averted its warmth from the naivety of globalism. Cultural differences are not for the High Street or questionable attempts at political control – one faction or another will always take hold, while peace remains a concept in the heart of John Lennon.

Multiculturalism is hard to realise – you can make a soup bowl of its untidy broth, but you cannot drink it with a forked tongue that balances clarity and love with slight of hand. The street of politics is where civil wars begin, with murmurings, whisperings and whitewashed doubt. Wars that seep out from the hearts of towns – those that feel suddenly threatened or have come adrift – or pull on their moorings like uncomfortable ships. Towns like these store the remains of love: hidden down dark cellar steps or boxed in the quiet of the attic above. Or in the biscuit tin stash that rules our empathy, where they are sealed with a sense of displacement and loss. These towns endure with their shoelaces undone – always likely to trip over the scourge of false virtue.

My home town went adrift a while ago and is now an uneasy place of talk and mistrust. And yes, it is pulling at its mooring ropes like a savage dog that soft thinking will not put down. A man died from tension – to do with race. His community (that should never have been regarded a separate place) marched down the street waving their cherished flag – spitting in the face of British hospitality. This was shown on the news with subversive relish, as the main stream media still exist on fractured loyalties – their editors, stirring the broth of death with unbalanced, divisive, censorious tools. It was

continued...

an insult to a friendly nation – a country that would rather hang its own, than allow a stranger to feel unwelcome, or to feel alone.

It would certainly hang the murderers of that victim, but the liberal-minded would also hang our better men, those who disagree with their grovelling stance – they have become renegade tools – these dilute liberals with nazi hearts, all in response to a fear for their own freedoms, that they now, in frenzy, tear apart.

Any man's death diminishes me, but they insist on spreading oil on a vulnerable sea. Playing games with people's lives that lead to wandering kitchen knives. It is an experiment played on *'lesser men' – the public – the you – the them.*

Britain has a history of self-deprecation, which is a symptom of cultural suicide. It comes from all quarters of the *English* soul, where freedom of speech is accompanied by hecklers who have nothing to do but shout themselves down.

4

part four

Return of the Nightwatchman

XXIV
What I hate About Feeling Fascistic

Attempt peace without idealism.

Good morning liberals. I am feeling rather fascist today and I am sorry to have to feel this way. Most sorry because I think you are foolish, especially on miserable fascist days like these – days born in the mirror of your reflected hatred; with those negative feelings you pretend not to entertain, but seem to have in reliable abundance – days when I have to rise into my mirror, unkind as a storm cloud, an unlikable fella – a fascist face – miserable as a sinner's wink.

I have become a creature; surely painted-on while I slept? Do not deny that you have been active again – sucking at the peaceful drops of night with venomous lips – scratching at my glass with accusing fingers – scribbling a Hitler moustache beneath my nose with a black-hearted pen. You are the goodly demons – good at labelling innocent men in your witch-hunt of spite, power and revenge.

continued...

I cannot decide whether to shave or cut my throat... or grow a beard and become a holy man? I would hold you hostage to your own pledge of tolerance, until you shut those lips that spout offence and learn to speak for truth instead. Yes, you have offended me – this fledgling holy man with a new beard. I am upset beyond God, and branded in the fire of what your so-called freedoms say. It would be difficult to kill myself with a plastic razor, but I will have a go, just to lend some cheer to your dark work. I suppose I could snap it in half and use the shards, or just carve a swastika into my shaved head – save you overburdening your withered library of derogatory words – let us leave them unsaid.

You can call me 'racist' instead – just to be absurd, though it would be in spite of my true beliefs, that are more complex and caring than your simple, unthinking eyes. You cannot see the poison oozing out of the presents you left beneath the Christmas tree, but as a holy man I will be nothing but helpful, and like the fool of fools, I will be glad to support your argument of lies.

I sold you my jackboots decades ago; your face was every inch the smile, as you pulled them on to your stick legs – and marched off, babbling bile. I suppose I could give in to your insidious finger that you think points to a perfect truth, but I cannot bear to look like an appeaser waving the tradition of paper proof. Just aim your finger between my eyes, like the barrel of an imaginary gun, you low-level bombing bastards of war – lower than the lowest of right-wing scum. What peace comes from vicious mouths like yours? Wide, sneering slits of self-righteous gore. I am sick of your whimpering through limited words that are cheap and easy and explain nothing. You want to be both sides of everything – the bat and the ball. You yearn for peace at any price, failing to understand that unfounded peace always brings the penalty of genocide or war – when you have weakened our walls with a violent wind that blows its serious chill to the front door.

I am sick of your wars, where we, the warriors, must die on behalf of your mistaken fears. You pretend to be doves, but you are psychotic hawks, tearing at the carrion of your people's love. You are the new, treacherous nazis in all you do – you are the insidious handshake in an unstable glue.

XXV
Jackboots and Red Shoes

History is repeating itself, though somewhat in disguise.
It travels incognito with subterfuge and lies...

1 : All Colours are Wrong

But the reds and whites are in Europe now and are poised to fight in their familiar fashion. And there are other complications too – used as decoys to stretch it out – those tools of slang and primitive re-invention. Did you vote to leave a political convention? Or did you try to stabilise an overreaching point of view? I think they turned old Europe upside down and shook you to the back of the queue. They were looking for stray ideas where there was previously only a history of tears, and the long-term uncertainty of doubt. They are painting Europe red now – they are painting it out – but not in the ideal of communist tastes – red for blood is the new design – a tint of bureaucracy and the endless race. It is all red tape and potential death – feeding a police state with some whining breath. And coming soon to a street near you, is its confusion of flags, its tear gas and a jackboot disguised as a shoe.

They will kick your teeth in –
make mince meat out of you.
They will have your guts for garters
while you throw some benign tomatoes
that slide off their shields like stew.

II : The End of Cliches

If I were you – trapped inside a machine of cogs, I would reassemble your countries from within. Try to start again, without suspect bandwagons – you could even attempt to start with a glorious 'anew', but only if you do not need cliché words from the shelves of poetry – stolen by a left wing point of view. Or is it the vile ache of political voice you yearn? A well payed life, leading to nowhere but concern? Prepare to sew-shut the eyes of the other view, and welcome more fruit-cakes to the lure of madness:

"Let us eat fruitcake!" will be our rallying cry. Merely mastering racial psychology will never do.
Any words, spat out in anger, will be rounded up like

continued...

dusty cattle – herded out of town and cancelled by silence. Soon they will measure race only by tears. There will be no other collateral in support of equality, or any that suits the media and their mercurial ways. They will measure employment by funding pain, and by developing international social aid, but only inside the rules of anger. There will be no other gauge of trusted certainty, and the rich will hang on to their stolen percentage. Markets will limp in the wreckage of oscillation, adopting cute graphs showing greed and hunger. All triggering the false courage of wayward thought, and all playing their infamous and awful game – it is the gamble that keeps the world apart – prevents the poor from noticing they are not regarded in strategy – only in the forfeit of blame.

The jackboot is on the left foot now, and there is a cauldron in Brussels where they melt down your flags. They forge them anew in perfect sky blue – throwing in gold stars to attract idealists. These symbols of vanity represent *chains of office*, and are drawn in a modern form of covert slavery. It is designed to fetter the *new world order* – made implicit by a false sense of paradise.

XXVI
Performance Poets

Performance Poets – Part One.

Performance poets are the worst. They are undeveloped and stoop in the corner of a mind. They frame themselves in some sort of now, grown old by the end of the mesmerising week. Unless they live fixed, intransigent lives, which they often do. Then they lace up that same old shoe. Worse still, they claim their poetry is adrift and has taken some sort of beating in a mill, or has slid away in an unexpected turn – become part of an obsequious queue – an alternative route, without form or scenery – an unstable gyroscope with a government grant – a scaffolding of phrases with over-tightened bolts. You can hear the dead words creaking in the noose. It is as though the passing years (now caked in truth) are not to do with the sun-stroked heads that grew in malice, to usurp the conscience of their youth.

They want us all to begin again – but just set forward by

continued...

an hour or two – and with a zero year to start us off – they are a fat-headed Pol Pot manipulating the history queue. They want to smash your head against a tree and press peanuts into your prying eyes, setting the funeral tone of past words to a notable grey scooped from the dark surprise... you can hear it cracking in the apocalyptic fire that is all too ready to burn its stubble. They throw words at the air like Pollock with paint, just to see what happens in the struggle. Or perhaps an abstract, accidental rhyme that they could then publicly hate? Or will they forget air and paper and write callous words on the muscles of their fate? Flexing them live – using breathing skin, having signed for it first with a stubby finger. Such weapons cannot write their own worth – they attended the lousiest school in the universe – its ancient sinews still patrol – or linger.

They are clouded souls, full of contempt – the tattooed skin that left their parents – a hair full of headbands and sketchy expectations, each echoing the ungracious train of heretical words – those perpetual proclamations – filtered through the motives of a grin.

These words are spat out promptly with a pat on the

back, delivered by pursuance and its feverish limp. They freed electricity to out-perform them, and soon there were flashing lights for a spent word's nominal credence – a reciprocal move that benefitted neither, so they promised to be dynamic – or at least eager – or something else – some kind of leaderless leader.

"The joke is behind you!" shout the drinking audience, joining in.

Or maybe just adopting a reluctant praise from a town in the North with coal-blackened sin? All this is more a hobby, or a discipline. They may as well be flying a kite as shouting O Captain! My Captain! Where do we begin?

Is your favourite poet a fake DJ, or a living room space with a human pulse? Their voices tighten like a knot, trying to hold onto sounds without generous aspect – sounds that live, more in the whim of a march – or in the automatic status of imagined roots. It is a pegged accent that can't be heard, just short of the detriments of gullible rap – a language developed in some ancient city street, where it became both ransacked and culprit in the same breath – providing easy access to nothing.

XXVII
Performing Live From a Book
Performance Poets – Part Two.

I am playing live tonight – you can hear me through the crack in the door; you can hear my spine crack as I straighten my tie; you can hear me tuck my shirt into my belt...

and sigh.

I play to the mirror first, to see if there is any improvement I could bear, or any hint of decrepitude I should not ignore that might, just for originality's sake, seem rare. Age is not an illness though – more like an avatar on the go. We parody our former looks into a lucid square, while he, the noble mirror, seals the windows and combs our hair... dragging us out, feet first onto the staged gravity of a cold and unforgiving stare.

He moans about how lined I look, and tired too, but worse, he points out my ageing eyelids and that I probably need a nurse. He is also disparaging about what he calls: 'my geriatric verse'. Perhaps I should be in care? Or at least... the very least, I might qualify for a chair; the way I groan when getting up, or take too long to open a door – or forget to close it fully shut. The mirror hears my sighs, they are a draft in his silvered heart. I fear he will shut me out one day – smashed to pieces, or he might depart. I would be a man without reflection then – a finally unplayable – wretched part.

At half-time, he peels the orange of my concerns and hands the slices out to anyone left with open ears; feeding a less than gracious audience with little shards of fruitful doubt, who all now realise the awful truth – that undeniable pear-shaped proof – that I have outwitted the reflection I was hung on before, and become that most popular of national treasures – the semi-lucid tumbleweed trainer – the monumental bore.

XXVIII
Poetry Has its Own Punctuation
Performance Poets – Part Three.

No fancy wordplay, please, it is over-done; it is a card-trick of the human mind. I have enough on my plate with real emotions – you should get some – without them, you are unkind. They drill through my head like goose feathers – I mean *loose letters – loose letters* – trying to form words of their own. I have no idea why I said *goose feathers*, or what I was thinking; should I have referenced them at all? I suppose they are holy things and can write with ink. I think they once wrote letters to the Vatican – arguing the elaborate validation of the most treasured Kink – and also to various, famous and decisive men – or maybe just scribbled a footnote in the bible of a nun? Or looking back, reminded the future what to think – and what might be done. Or maybe it was carved from the bone that your teacher said was a genuine rib from a Rolling Stone? We will never know that here, attending in our many thousands – yet completely alone.

They keep the bones of saints inside vaults of stone and in times of issue, listen to see if they move. But I do not want to listen to your silent groove, so move your microphone to 'Goose Head Soup' – to a track that gets its letters wrong and gets your goat as well. Especially in your trite facades of vague nobility. It is not much different from evensong – so long, so long with your evensong – and with your purposeless accented tones, each carrying words as impenetrable as the guardian-fringe of Brian Jones.

I have already alleged – cruelty to poetry – while you were gutting a fish in your simple insanity, and your heart was reciting poems in the form of a wish while the sea asked for this injustice to be returned. So where are we now in this mindless muddle? Where is home for the man in the middle? Nothing is found by searching low – just leave a full stop in the air and go.

XXIX
Measured in Murmurs

Performance Poets – Part Four.

I am sitting with a coffee amongst the murmurings of people, a stone's throw from my own insanity. I will murmur too in a moment, but I will murmur on my own terms – a leaking balloon – reluctant to die.

Solo murmuring is not permitted here – not without uncomfortable looks bursting with suspicion, or a carefully controlled smile with a guarded derision. This stoop will vibrate between awkward comrades, all around this mercenary café of belligerent sitters. With a flick of heads and a quick eye – or the concerned stirring of a thinking spoon.

It is forbidden here to step beyond the skin, or make any utterance without a designated receiver. Someone negatively charged – able to unhitch the cart of potential doom or defuse the sweating fuse, dripping with gelignite. Someone to catch my thoughts and bat them back, especially if accompanied by a range of sounds. In my case, lost sounds from the screaming deep of Edvard Munch – mouthed, but unthreatening – and of the past.

People are unnerved by sound, and will only trust themselves to agreed parameters – after that, they will test the air like disturbed deer and shy away. I too had friends once – many of them. I travelled with people, both men and women. We talked and laughed, just like you. And looking back from this unique distance, it was all done in a cloud of murmurs too. So be careful what you think of me – you are in the presence of an impersonating cuckoo, and this style of lip is the only voice I know. I can easily reconstruct these lost friends, when all have gone inside their breath. I am one who lives amongst the refuge of treasured memories and the gift of stars. I refuse to believe that what is done is gone. Are there still spiders on Mars?

You too will be alone one day, but I... I will always be the resurrection of someone – in the presence, the beauty and the sound of all those I knew – now gone, it's true, but I will reach out with a murmur...

and stop the setting sun.

XXX
A Period Of Talking Heads

Performance poets – Part Five.

We are living in an age of avatars – squared representations, flanking text and images. They are our soul on record – our dust, settled to form an empirical being – in a signed thumbprint.

In the art world, styles of avatars vary – from proud reproductions of personal triumph, to anonymous images made of ideas or crayons. These fantasies are homages to transient gods, or the simple baggage of a lauded fool. In poetry, avatars are mostly portraits, wilting with ambition – or with a haunted expression, featuring the aspiring laureate with a discerning look – as though a talent of pure vapour would do poetry any good. Sometimes, there is a hint of loose dishonesty, or a conceit of glamour – something to fall back on when the poems turn sour – when they have dropped their leaden letters through the silence of a reader's ice, and there is only the trivia of hype left to work the words.

In practicality, faces have become initial letters, as though some combination of expression had never introduced soft words to hard edges – never seen a line-up of aspiring hopefuls, or the 'chosen group' of likely scribes. I will not condemn them as 'usual suspects', but they are... in their cliched way... or maybe just an exotic name, with its fresher unguent, wafted from afar.

There are more poets per square page than love-song leaves falling from an autumn guitar, but this is how it should be told, so autumn can take care of its precious hold of rusting words – its homeward fall. Slicing with a scything wind – and ruthlessly – and with a gentle, but firm goodbye to most, if not all. There are always old, bruised apples though, that hang, fat to the delicious tree, defying descent, or swept into piles for the final scrutiny of death's redemption.

These precious heads need say little; the talking dead heads say much more: name; address; status of loneliness; intention of mediocrity; or less; and a profound interest in written trivia, learned in a class and

continued...

told by fools. These eternal-neophytes, with one hand on the rules, who lecture their way through the neat years – are still afloat – like empty vessels, leeching into a tumid river – quoting Eliot and Dylan Thomas and ignoring the shiver of the flanking forest – a foliage, full of closed eyes in radial contempt. They ignore the depths beneath their bloated schools, where the lurking minds of students sink, before swaggering home to the unkept secrets of popular tunes.

Eventually, some teacher words will splatter out a page of blood – a sudden attack of tuberculosis, spilling from a history of the neighbourhood. Then they will call themselves poets – at last – and remove the sterilising teacher's-hood – these un-sinking souls, blessed with paradise, yet losing in the game and about to mess up.

They think they are bearing their cornered souls by revealing they took sugar in the tar of expresso – or did – a while ago, stubbing out cigarettes during a live performance, in the trite essence of a garden shed... when they first lusted to become a photographic square in the back of a perfect book.

XXXI
The Cake of Peace

Let us confound the powers that be
and decide to live in peace.

Peace is hypnotic. It makes you think that war is over. Makes you wonder how nations get to killing each other, just from a squabble about some land, or a river, or a dead king, that now seem hardly worth the bother. Especially now these nations are friendly again and happy with their wine and beer and shared art – that intellectual nobody, peering around its pretentious corner.

During peace, nations put the kettle on and fall in love; distracted by the thin veneer of unreliable memories. Blessed with children, they build an environment of playful noise, where reasons are forgotten and nothing truly matters. The world becomes a soft madness then, where advertising takes over from reason – icing the new cake with expendable shoes.

This is the cake of peace. It lives in your pantry and

continued...

survives your guests. You peer at it weekly, to make sure it is unsliced and still holds the promises devised in the treaty. Meanwhile, the next enemy will have their foot in the door and an eye on your cake. They will have stolen the march on the world's slippered feet.

Europe is easy pickings and so is our cake – we baked it sweet and it is tempting. Even camouflage netting cannot hide it from desire; there is an arrow to the heart of their rigorous campaign. First they try to divide our cake and invade our peace, but they are clumsy, like the traditional dolts all enemies must be – and we start to kill them, with the liberal warning that we will not attempt to burst their skin. They are at once encouraged and offended by our weakness; they ignore our indifference and continue to slice our cake of peace. It is confusion like this, that makes politics crumble – spilling into the distraction of available war.

Once in a while, war rolls in on a more dangerous tide. Less about cake than megalomania and genocide. Look out for the signs – almost half your population will have its head in the sand, while speaking muffled grumbles with a mouth full of cake – *The Cake* – that cake of peace, now imprudently shared out in the folly of appeasement – spoken in crumbs and almost gone.

Governments will refuse to admit that the art of peace is their supposed work – believing their commitment is only to be at war. They have reached this conclusion by the peaceful decisions of broken democracy, which they blame you for – not using your vote correctly in the face of the enemy.

For the process of war, they will need your help to fight their battles and close the pantry door – even though it was they who left it open, on a birthday spent welcoming fools. There will be a bigger cake then – and more expensive, with oddly threatening, yet delicious details –

"A waste of money and lives," some will say.
But this is the cake of war – it is armoured with icing-sugar and has a gun.

XXXII
The Pig Fat Revolution: June 2016

Part One; The death of parliamentary democracy.

The Sun shone that day on a brighter Britain. One I had not seen in many years. A Britain where people regained confidence and hope – the smiling Sisyphus, refusing to be foiled by the sly media's slippery slope – that brainwashing pool of subliminal soup that still simmers lukewarm, between fact and fake – and that appeases the weary minds of tired men and the growing pains of the vulnerable young.

Political news had become a sermon; an instruction; a cigarette of insidious addiction; an icing sugar of arsenic from sweet, lying lips. They offered templates to mask our fear of the things we needed to fear most. They urged responsibility and decried betrayal, while pointing as guilty lambs, elsewhere. They sought to numb our brains and change our view, threatening virtue with a mercenary stare – but a whispered smoke from liberal lungs gave them away, blown on the breath of these militant clowns – still pretending to be you. The government and opposition had pushed its imperious head out too far and we removed it with a democratic vote – along with their pig-headed leader's snout. We killed his swineherd too; killed them for governing the demise of democracy towards the facile era of the unelected European lout. Ours was a democracy, very much alive – a democracy of delinquency, they had accidentally let slip out. Their sausage machine of globalist thought, with its thin veneer and its dubious glue had fallen apart. They had it coming – those wastrel pigs and their blood-stained brothers in the European sty. It was a pig fat coup, addressed to the future of hope and freedom – a raising of the arm against the federal lie.

Suddenly, there were rivers of molten fat running down the ornaments of Westminster Palace – yet still rather Puginesque, I thought, with their fine, sliding fingers of candle wax. It was the flame of democracy, newly ignited by a clear and more hopeful light. One that shone beyond the mouthed windows of parliament with the brighter power of awakened hearts. It shone beyond the ornamental ways and the cracks of countless window panes, through which the assuming eyes of politicians

continued...

had never thought to gaze – not without a superior introspection – and not until that day, in the summer of hope... yes, they saw us then, through fat smeared windows – they were never good with clarity, so they saw us perfectly well – an unworthy nuisance – in their tired truth of blistered vision. And that is all we were to them anyway – an awkward blur – a gang of no one.

And they still wonder who we are now – we, who have slain them and shut them up; sealed their menace inside a London tomb, their exotic bubble of privilege, orchestrated failure, recovery and boom. A capital that has shamed its country – departing for elsewhere like a broken leper – an unplaced jigsaw of unfocussed ideals that should have worked to see the British viewpoint better – in a balanced state that held some dignity. There were a few picture postcard scenes, held in fixity by cheap labour promises and hidden champagne – the libations of rich and unseen men – pretending to represent social deprivation and pain.

The Westminster lawn was full of bodies then. The media had died of microphones and feedback – a squealing fuel that held truth in stasis, while paid voices shouted the rest of it down. It was a triumphant silence of paraphernalia as we made them eat the propaganda of their edited words.

They had their chance to listen to us, but refused, preferring to preach a simplistic denial – a denial of democracy and of what we 'the people' said. It was a cynical retort, concocted in a smothering cocoon and spoken with a panicked breath:

"This is not what you meant to say," they said. "And besides, we've gone deaf."

That was their arrogant interpretation of a living breath – along with various threats and warnings of dread: the third world war; the Armageddon –

"For God's sake, we will run out of bread!"

All these tamperings were over-emphasised in a stirred and stirring media heat. Even the American President stooped from singing jazz, to threaten the actual concept of democracy with a back seat.

Ours was a revolution of freedom and choice, not just something different to do because we could. Something coded news words had no letters for – they had used them all in the weave of an imaginary truth – using

continued...

stuffed-up, awkward words with inbuilt pledges – such as 'unity', 'security' and 'integration' – all of which drove into our national hearts like wedges.

By then, we had built our respective ghettos to shut the madness out – that deafening sound of manipulation which descended into whisperings of contagious doubt. Or the hissing leech of globalisation, that boiled below its legitimate veneer, like an old sweat-shop staffed with slaves from anywhere but here. It was fit for nothing, except its time to implode – and its time to implode was already here.

They had engineered a small Earth of unspeakable tension, labelling it multicultural diversity instead, all while trying to make those two tired words a convention – crossed-eyes, pushed into the same head – a bridge; and awning; a failed umbrella. We had all huddled beneath its wilderness of graffiti and inevitable terror. For this was the end of Babylon – the end of the road, via a corrupt prejudice of their own making – their indifference to any race, culture or colour. They had sought to make each numbered human a customer – each demographic life a market thread – there for the chasing, these citizens from anywhere – some with enthusiastic spending power, stepping into the shoes of our not quite dead. When we finally got our letters back, the words of the day were 'democracy' and 'hope' both offering freedom and choice but with actual choice and a true sense of hope. Freedom of speech restored to barred lips.

In this new moment of national therapy, the word 'democracy' had begun again, with that true balance decided by the people, instead of being cast like dice for the goals of mercenary and faceless men. It caught on too, like a giddy fool – forced as it was, from reluctant lips, who suddenly loved the idea of democracy, like it was a new toy for greed and investigation. They wanted to play with it – relentlessly – until it worked only in their own employ.

Part Two; There is no part One.

They still believe they can preach a reversal. I can hear their insidious collusions with the media mouth, quietly ticking in the raked-over embers of a stunned silence in the sulking south. I can smell a curling whiff of liberal

continued...

smoke creeping up the fraying edges where these first candles were lit – these candles of joy and wonderful hope now lapsing into the trauma of being snuffed out. The invisible paymasters have decreed it so, with a disregarded empathy and the vast greed of controlling wealth – but what fool and his money dare tamper with democracy in the shifting sands of an enlightened world? What scoundrels will snub the deep-felt cry of those expressing the call of liberty – that righteous demand that truth – and you and I – and even pigs might fly?